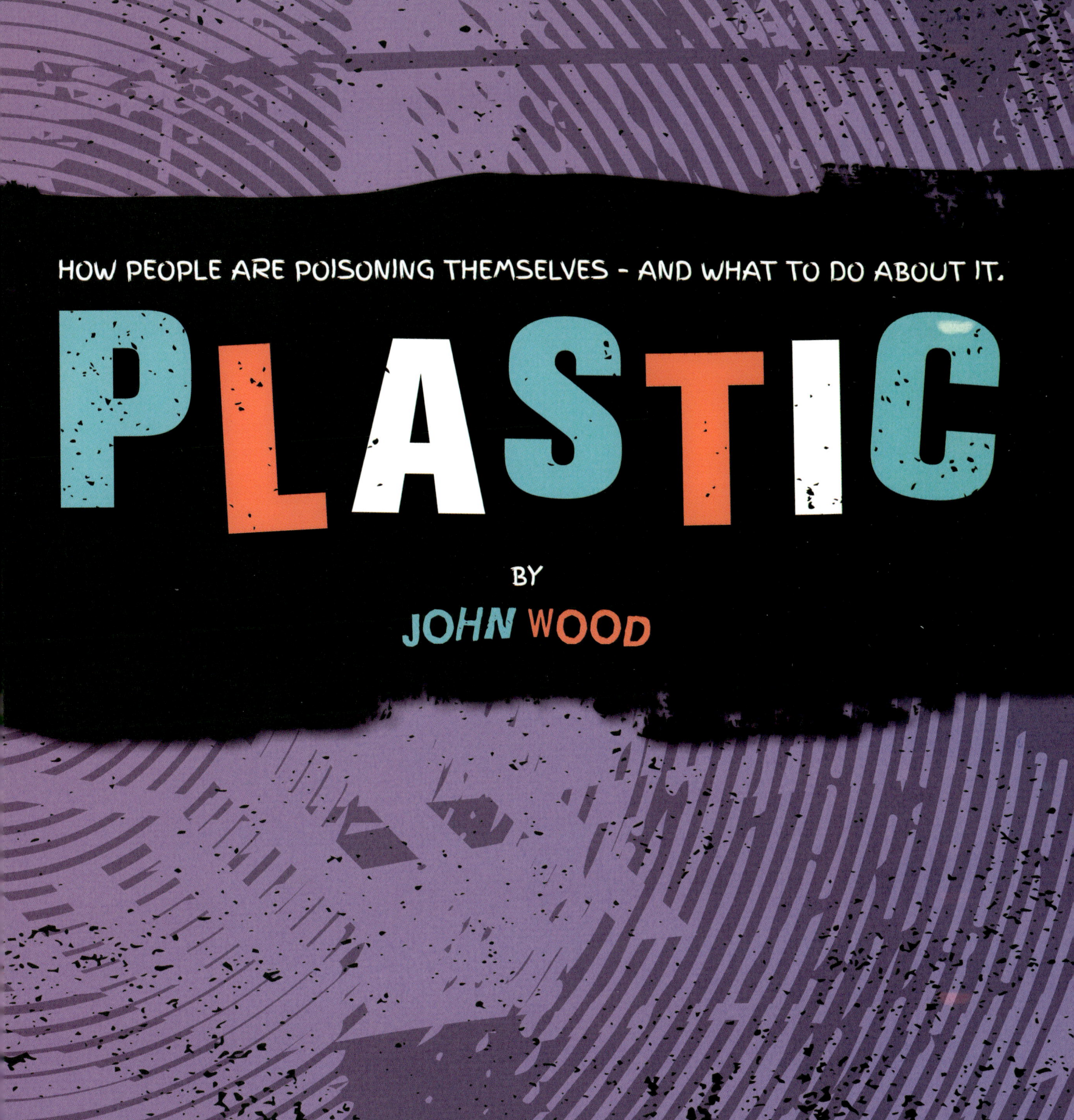

BookLife PUBLISHING

©2021
BookLife Publishing Ltd.
King's Lynn
Norfolk PE30 4LS

All rights reserved.
Printed in Malta.

A catalogue record for this book is available from the British Library.

ISBN: 978-1-83927-456-5

Written by:
John Wood

Edited by:
William Anthony

Designed by:
Danielle Rippengill

All facts, statistics, web addresses and URLs in this book were verified as valid and accurate at time of writing. No responsibility for any changes to external websites or references can be accepted by either the author or publisher.

Image Credits

All images are courtesy of Shutterstock.com, unless otherwise specified. With thanks to Getty Images, Thinkstock Photo and iStockphoto. Cover: wow.subtropica, Rayyy, sokolovski, Milan M, Teerasak Ladnongkhun, Tinnakorn jorruang. Images used on every page – Rayyy, wow.subtropica. 4 – Khrystofor. 5 – LadyPhotos. 6 – MOHAMED ABDULRAHEEM. 7 – M.Somchai. 8 – Willyam Bradberry. 9 – Larina Marina. 10 – Again Peace. 11 – vwPix. 12 – Erlantz P.R. 13 – anyaivanova. 14 – Karel Bartik. 15 – Olha Rohulya, Rudmer Zwerver, Anan Kaewkhammul. 16 – Sundry Photography. 17 – Najmi Arif. 18 – Jao Cuyos. 19 – oneinchpunch. 20 – wavebreakmedia. 21 – Aleksandra Suzi. 22 – Huw Penson. 23 – Wutthichai Phosri.

CONTENTS

PAGE 4 Plastic Everywhere
PAGE 6 The Problem with Plastic
PAGE 8 Polluting the Sea
PAGE 10 What Is Microplastic?
PAGE 14 The Food Chain
PAGE 16 An Invention to Clean the Seas
PAGE 18 Getting Plastic out of the Ocean
PAGE 20 Stop Plastic Pollution!
PAGE 24 Glossary and Index

Words that look like this can be found in the glossary on page 24.

PLASTIC EVERYWHERE

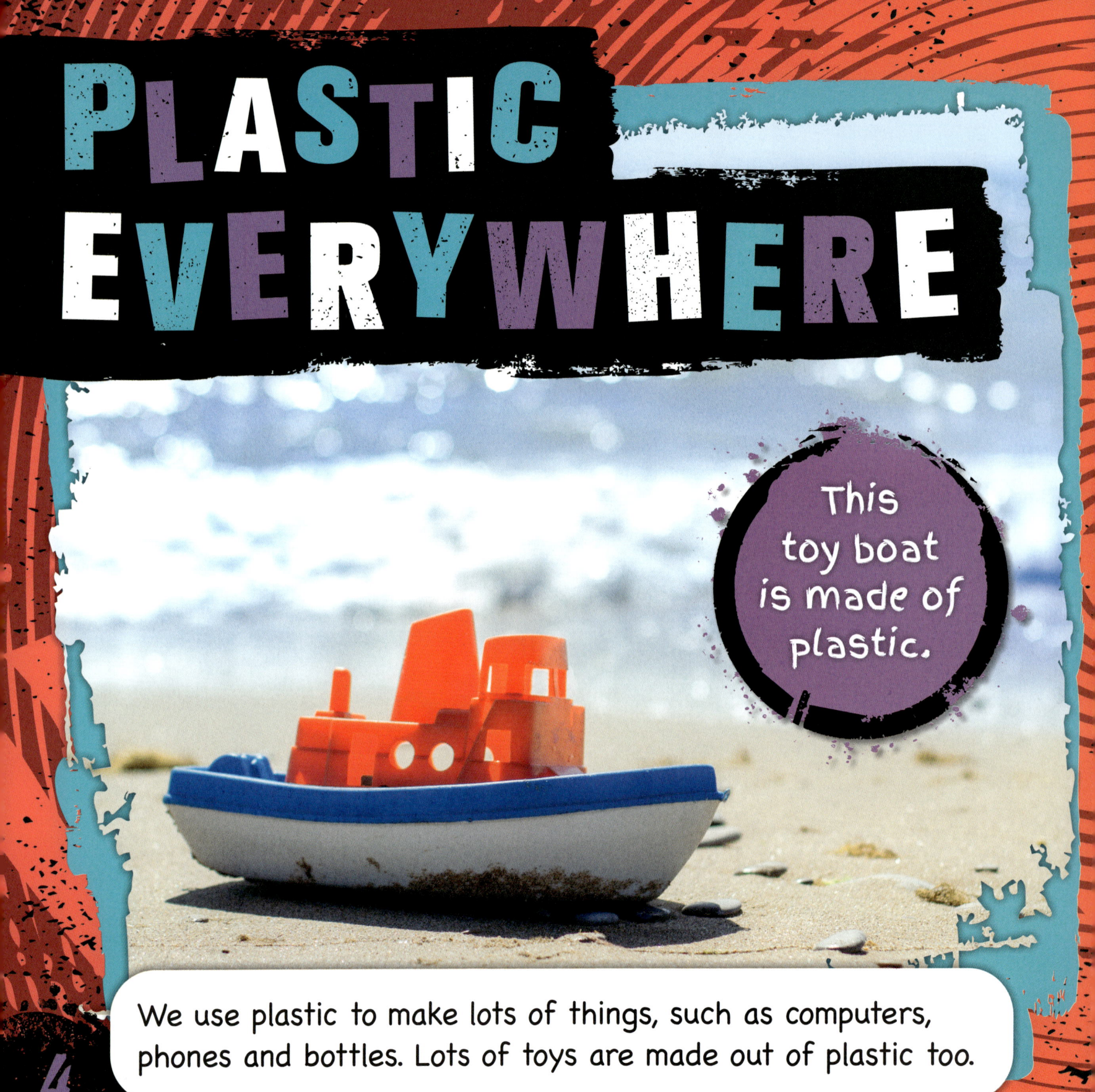

This toy boat is made of plastic.

We use plastic to make lots of things, such as computers, phones and bottles. Lots of toys are made out of plastic too.

Plastic is very useful. Sometimes it is made to be soft, like a plastic bag. It can also be hard, like plastic forks and spoons. But where does plastic go when we are done with it?

Plastic can be see-through, or it can be colourful like these plastic chairs.

The PROBLEM with PLASTIC

This landfill is full of plastic.

If plastic is not recycled properly, it can be very bad for the planet. Plastic doesn't completely break down and go away. This is a problem when it is dumped in landfill or in the ocean.

All this plastic causes big problems for animals. They might get tangled in the plastic and become trapped, or accidentally eat it and die.

A monkey trapped in a plastic bag

POLLUTING the SEA

Lots of plastic ends up in the ocean. It can break into smaller and smaller pieces and become dangerous to all the animals.

A turtle might eat a plastic bag because they think it is a jellyfish. This can choke them.

Lots of plastic washes up on beaches too.

If an animal gets trapped in plastic, it can make it harder to find food and survive. Pieces of plastic can also get stuck in the animal and hurt them.

WHAT IS MICROPLASTIC?

Microplastic

When plastic breaks down into very small pieces, smaller than five millimetres, it is called microplastic. Microplastic is very dangerous to animals and people.

Microbeads are another type of microplastic. Microbeads are added to things such as toothpaste or face washes. However, these small microbeads can get into the ocean and can be eaten by small animals.

Microplastic has been found everywhere in the world, from the highest mountain to the deepest point in the ocean. Not only is plastic dangerous for animals, but it could be dangerous to people too.

Every year, 8 million tonnes of plastic are put into the ocean.

Plastic has been found in over 100 species in oceans, seas and rivers.

Scientists still don't know how bad microplastic is to humans.

Microplastic is sometimes too small to see. It is in the water we drink, the air we breathe and the food we eat. Plastic can leak chemicals into the ground, or into our food and water.

Plastic pollution is found throughout the food chain. But what is a food chain?

The FOOD CHAIN

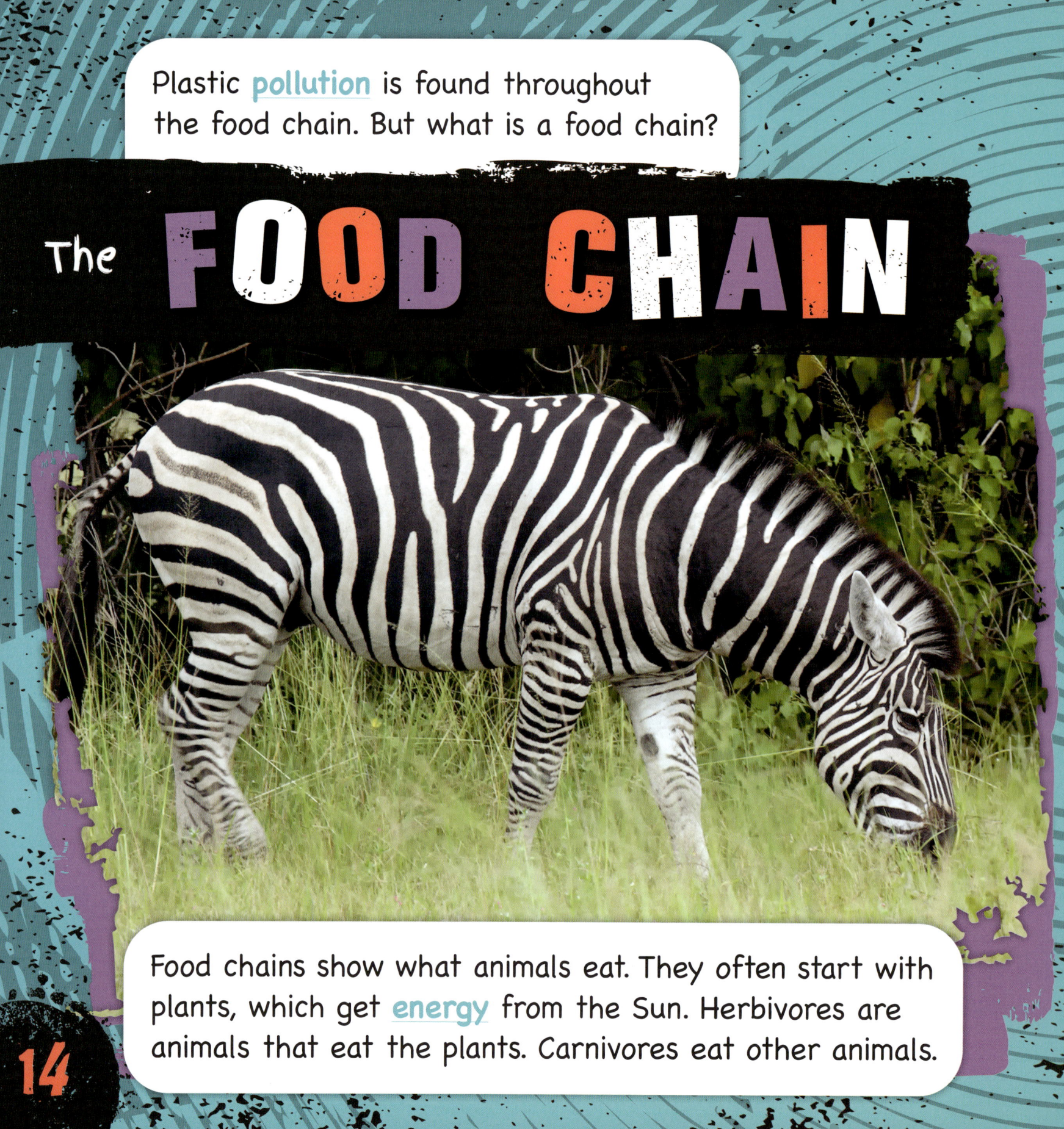

Food chains show what animals eat. They often start with plants, which get energy from the Sun. Herbivores are animals that eat the plants. Carnivores eat other animals.

Here is a simple food chain you might find in the woods.

Fruit from a plant

Mouse

Owl

Animals might eat plants and other animals with plastic inside them. This is how microplastics travel up the food chain. This can be bad for people because we are part of the food chain too.

An INVENTION to CLEAN the SEAS

An Ocean Cleanup project boat

The Ocean Cleanup project uses an invention that looks like a giant floating barrier. The barrier drifts along the waves, collecting plastic which will eventually be taken out of the sea by boats.

So far, the Ocean Cleanup project is mainly trying to clean an area of the Pacific Ocean known as the Great Pacific Garbage Patch.

The Great Pacific Garbage Patch is an island of rubbish that is three times the size of France.

This is called the Interceptor, and it is cleaning up a river in Asia.

GETTING PLASTIC OUT of the OCEAN

Inventions such as the ones used by the Ocean Cleanup project are very good at collecting big pieces of plastic. However, small pieces of plastic are a lot harder to clean up.

These people are picking plastic off the beach to recycle it instead.

It is important to act quickly to clean up our world. We need to use less plastic and make sure it is recycled or thrown away properly.

STOP PLASTIC POLLUTION!

You could also see if there are any eco-friendly projects at school that you can join in with.

Here are some things you can do to help stop plastic pollution and keep this planet clean and safe.

Make sure you recycle as much plastic as you can. Ask a grown-up if you are unsure whether something can be recycled or not.

You might have different bins for recycling at home.

Try not to use plastic at all! Ask your grown-ups to buy reusable bags instead of plastic bags. Can you get paper straws instead of plastic ones? Can you think of any other plastic that could be replaced?

These toothbrushes are made of bamboo.